# THE FIRE PHOENIX

BY
Penny Stempel

This edition first published by Parragon Books Ltd in 1995

Produced by
Magpie Books Ltd, London

Illustrations courtesy of: Rex Features

ISBN 0 75250 725 7

A copy of the British Library Cataloguing in Publication
Data is available from the British Library.

Typeset by Hewer Text Composition Services, Edinburgh
Printed in Singapore by Printlink International Co.

It is just after 1a.m., 31 October, the morning of Hallowe'en. The stage door of the Viper Club, latest haunt of the Hollywood young and beautiful, is thrown open. A young man with short black hair, Converse sneakers and jeans is carried out by two young women and a man. Out cold, he looks in a bad way. But this is Sunset Strip and early morning revellers have seen it all before. They pass on by. They don't yet know what is soon to be splashed across front pages and broadcast on every channel: River Phoenix, twenty-three-year-old star, loved by the camera, the eco-conscious and teenage girls worldwide, is dying, right there on the sidewalk.

The Viper lies on the corner of Larrabee Street and Sunset Strip. Co-owned by Johnny Depp – star of *Edward Scissorhands* – and old rocker Chuck Weiss, it lies a stone's throw from the Whisky, the Roxy and Tatou. Freelance photographer Ron Davis, snapper of the rich and famous, was there that night. And what he saw was seared into his memory, to replay again and again. River Phoenix, the serious and clean-living star, was carried out of the club by the film actress Samantha Mathis, who was River's girlfriend, and by Joaquin (a.k.a. Leaf) Phoenix, River's younger brother. There was another woman with them, Rainbow Phoenix, River's twenty-

year-old sister. River looked drunk, he
was liquid in their arms. He flopped to the
ground and then the seizures started, first
one, then another. His eyes were rolled
back in his head, his arms were flailing,
flying up and down. Rainbow lay on top
of River, trying to suppress the move-
ment. After the fifth seizure he went still.
Later, all America was to hear his brother's
anguished 911 call played over and over
on radio and TV: 'My brother's having
seizures. I'm thinking he had Valium or
something. You must get here, please,
because he's dying.'

Five minutes later, when the four-strong
paramedics team arrived, Phoenix had 'no
pulse and was not breathing'. They gave
basic life-support and then lifted him into
an ambulance. At 1.51a.m., after twenty
minutes in the emergency room of the
Cedars-Sinai Medical Centre a few blocks

south, River Phoenix was officially declared dead. But those who saw him on the Sunset Strip pavement have no real doubt that he died there, on a warm October night, under the curved black awning that protects departing Viper customers from rain that never falls. River Phoenix joined the pantheon of Hollywood stars whose image retains a special lustre because they never lived to grow old – James Dean, John Belushi, Marilyn Monroe – but he joined early. Phoenix lived two years less than James Dean, three less than Jean Harlow, eleven less than John Belushi.

The autopsy confirmed that there was Valium in River's system, and marijuana and ephedrine. But it was massive doses of heroin and cocaine that killed him, doses that, according to the coroner's office, would each have been lethal on its own.

There were no needle marks and no one knew how the drugs had been taken. Nor was anyone sure just when they were taken (drugs are metabolized at different rates by different people). But a routine police search of Phoenix's suite at the Nikko Hotel in West Hollywood after his death turned up Valium, heroin and cocaine.

Stunned Hollywood pundits asked how this could have happened to someone like River Phoenix, a sweet-faced golden boy whose passionate concerns were saving the rain forests and the humane treatment of animals. What was it that went so wrong for River?

# Nature's Child

The story begins in 1968, two years before the young star-to-be was born, and the year in which a twenty-two-year-old Jewish woman, a secretary called Arlyn Dunetz, left her husband and job in Manhattan to take her chances in California. Hitching one day on Santa Monica Boulevard, Los Angeles, with a friend, the pair were picked up by a man called John. John was born in Fontana, California. He was a year younger than Arlyn, had also been married before and had a daughter named Trust. Two days later they met up again and talked until early morning. They were, they discovered, both 'seekers', and decided they should travel together.

They took to the road, finding work as they could. In the summer of 1970 they were earning a living picking apples on a commune in Madras, Oregon, and it was there, on 23 August, that Arlyn gave birth to their first child, River Jude. River's name was inspired by the River of Life in Hermann Hesse's novel *Siddhartha*. It was a natural birth, and the child of mixed destiny was born in a log cabin to a roar of approval from friends invited by Arlyn to share in the experience.

John and Arlyn, still searching for meaning, now with their young child, continued to travel in the West. In Pikes Peak, Colorado, they found their purpose.

Joining up to the evangelical religious cult, the Children of God, they became missionaries for the group, first in Crockett, Texas, where their daughter Rain Joan of Arc was born in 1973, then further afield – in Mexico and Puerto Rico, where Arlyn gave birth to Joaquin. (Rain later changed her name to Rainbow, while Joaquin at the age of four adopted the name Leaf.) In Caracas, Venezuela, Libertad Mariposa, or Liberty Butterfly, was born. By now John was 'Archbishop of Venezuela and the Caribbean' for the Children of God.

But after two years' selfless work for the cult in South and Central America, John and Arlyn were rudely awoken from their dream. Magazines blew the Children of God apart. Leader David Berg, they revealed, was a fraud who recruited through sex. This was not the sanctuary from the hypocrisy and venality of mainstream

America that they had sought, and John and Arlyn split from the sect. This was the first occasion when the couple put their faith in false idols, and this time they were able to take their leave unscathed. The second was to prove fatal for their son, River.

John, Arlyn, River, Rain, Leaf and Liberty made ends meet as best they could, living in a beach hut in Venezuela and waiting for guidance from a 'Universal Being'. And it was now that the seeds were sown for River's future. River, aged five, and Rain, aged three, sang hymns and played religious songs on the streets of Caracas, in front of hotels or at the airport, to bring in money for the family. Much later, River was to tell the press, 'It was a great stepping-stone. I learned to play guitar there – my sister Rain and I got interested in performing. It was a neat time growing up in Venezuela in the late seventies.'

It was not until 1977 that the unorthodox family unit made their way back to the US. Inspired by a meeting with a doctor and ex-rock star, they stowed away on an old freighter that carried Tonka toys. The crew discovered them halfway there – four kids and a pregnant mother – threw a big party for them and gave them a load of toys. They settled in Florida, John worked as a gardener, and their youngest child, daughter Summer Joy, was born. To celebrate their new beginning, the clan took the name Phoenix. Their previous name became such a closely guarded secret that media attention has failed to uncover it.

# Fortune Seekers

In 1978, when Summer Joy was just three months old, John Phoenix injured his back. He could no longer work and there was no money. Alongside the spiritual rebirth, a new business plan was needed: the children were to earn. River and Rain, now nine and seven, began to perform in local talent contests, and River walked away with prize after prize. Arlyn became gripped by the conviction that her children could captivate the world. She mailed her old school pal Penny Marshall, star of the

River Phoenix

Caracas, Venezuela

TV comedy series *Laverne and Shirley*, cuttings about her talented offspring, and the response – a standard reply from the Head of Talent at Paramount – proved sufficient encouragement for the family to begin a new migration. In a shaky old car, the family took to the road and headed off to California to seek their show-business fortune. John Phoenix was later to recall, 'I said to myself: What a crazy person you are. But the stars were so bright. I just felt it had to be right.'

Arlyn Phoenix may have been a hippy, but she was a hard-nosed hippy nonetheless. While River's father John preferred his privacy, Arlyn was to be the driving force in her eldest son's career. Once in Hollywood, she got herself a job at NBC TV as secretary to the Head of Talent, at one blow securing herself both a crash-course in the entertainment business and wages. She stayed long enough to learn the ropes and then quit to push River. Step one was to secure agent Iris Burton to act for River and his four siblings. Burton had Phoenix on her books for most of his career from age nine. 'He was the most beautiful child you've ever seen, like a little Elvis,' she said.

Her first move was to put him forward for TV commercials. River was picked to promote Ocean Spray, Saks and Mitsubishi. But River always stressed that his parents sought and respected their children's view. When, at age ten, the young performer wanted to quit advertising work ('I felt', he said, 'that the constant lying, the smiling on cue and the product-naming was going to drive me crazy.'), his developing career was redirected and Phoenix hit the LA TV audition circuit.

The earnest and beguiling young actor continued his charmed progress. He played guitar on the daytime series *Fantasy*, he did audience warm-ups for the show *Real Kids*, and he played cheeky twelve-year-old Guthrie McFadden in twenty-two episodes of CBS's 1982 cattle saga *Seven Brides for Seven Brothers*. The jobs came thick and fast: in 1984 there was the NBC mini-series *Celebrity*, an after-school educational special *Backwards: The Riddle of Dyslexia*, and an NBC pilot *It's Your Move*; 1985 saw fifteen-year-old River as Robert Kennedy jun. in *Robert Kennedy and His Times*, a guest star in Michael J. Fox's long-running series *Family Ties*, and a lead part in ABC's *Surviving: A Family in Crisis*.

The boy Phoenix had conquered TV, but River was born to run and his next move was to the big screen. 'Some people find security in routine, but I could never live that way,' he said, and the dice was still loaded in his favour. His first movie, in 1985, was a science fiction adventure called *Explorers*. Picked from 4,000 boys nationwide, River played boffin Wolfgang Muller, a bespectacled boy genius who conjures up a spaceship in his lab and makes his friend's dreams come true. By the time he was fifteen, he had been professionally cute for more than five years. He was probably his family's chief breadwinner. He had never been to school.

If *Explorers* established Phoenix as a serious contender in Tinseltown, his next role, won in the same year, was one of three in his career – *Stand By Me, Running On Empty* and *My Own Private Idaho* – that touched closest to his own experience and won him unstinting critical acclaim. For

Rob Reiner's rites of passage movie *Stand By Me*, Phoenix was selected from over 300 youthful would-be stars to play thirteen-year-old Chris Chambers, the boy from the wrong side of the tracks.

*Stand By Me*, based on a Stephen King novella, chronicles one summer weekend in 1958 in the lives of four boys reaching adolescence. When the fat boy of the foursome overhears talk of a dead kid's body lying next to a railway track the friends make a pact to find the corpse, and the intimacy of the trail with its gruesome goal leads the boys to lay bare their fears and vulnerabilities to each other.

Like Phoenix's later directors, Reiner was a film-maker who searched for honesty, insisting on one week of improvisation before any work started on the script,

with the result that the onscreen rapport
between the four boys was real. River, in
particular, came up with the goods, and
Reiner commented, 'You just turned the
camera on and he would tell the truth'. As
a tough kid, hardened by his father's
beatings, dragging manfully on his cigar-
ettes, Phoenix gave a performance of
tenderness, honesty and older-than-his-
years wisdom as he offered guidance to
his young friends and faced out an older
gang of thugs (led by Kiefer Sutherland as
Ace) with courage. 'If I was your father,'
Chris Chambers tells tearful buddy Gor-
die, rejected by his father in favour of his
recently deceased older brother, 'things
would be different.' Phoenix – in real
life the oldest sibling in difficult circumstances – was always to be at his best on
screen when giving solace or voicing his
own pain. It was this fragile sensitivity that
made Phoenix ultimately unfit to with-

stand the multi-layered hypocrisies of Hollywood life. With typical humility, River said of this role: 'In *Stand By Me* I realized that what I was creating was going to live on far longer than anything of me as a person. The characters are more powerful than the person that creates them.' Little did he know how prophetic his words would be.

Phoenix's journey from boyhood to manhood apparently took place off as well as on screen. Co-star Corey Feldman claimed that both he and Phoenix experimented with marijuana for the first time during the shoot, while director Rob Reiner told of another first for Phoenix: 'He showed up to work one morning with a big smile on his face; the night before he'd lost his virginity. A friend of the family – I think she was about eighteen – took River out to the backyard where they tented out. He said, "She was very patient with me and showed me what to do." '

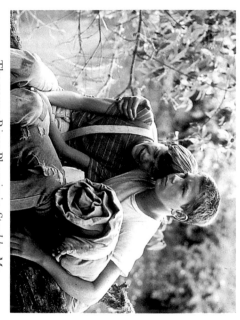

The young River Phoenix in *Stand by Me*

In *Mosquito Coast*

# A Healthy Attitude to Hollywood

When *Stand By Me*, a quirky, low-budget production initially given limited distribution, became a surprise hit and beat the Tom Cruise vehicle *Top Gun* to the number one slot, River Phoenix was a Hollywood name. He knew the dangers, but at fifteen had all the confidence of adolescence that he could withstand them. 'People say, the movie's so good, you're going to be the next this or the next that. Take it the wrong way and you can get really high on yourself,' said the young actor, unwittingly describing his own future. 'You get pampered, you hang out at a ritzy hotel, get room service at the snap of your fingers, or have a limo, which is really weird. You can change and it's sad.'

But for now, the sun was still shining and Phoenix's next movie gave him a lead role alongside a major star, Harrison Ford. It also brought inevitable comparisons with the boy-actor's own family history. In *The Mosquito Coast* (1986), directed by Australian Peter Weir (*Picnic at Hanging Rock, Witness*), Phoenix played elder son Charlie to Harrison Ford's mad inventor father, Allie Fox – the man whose mission to take his ice-machine to the Mosquito Coast turns him into a dictator who comes close to destroying his wife and family. Phoenix's Charlie was the film's narrator, and his relationship with his father the focus of the film as the boy comes to realize that his father's genius is flawed. Weir had cast Phoenix because of the similarity between Charlie and River's peripatetic, faith-led childhoods, and once again Phoenix played a wise child pitched against adversity, required to shore up his father's fragile ego as well as carrying the burden of his siblings and his mother.

When he saw the daily rushes, Weir knew he had made the right choice. 'When a big close-up would come on the screen, it was like you were a kid and you went to a film and you couldn't keep your eyes off a character. It's something apart from the acting ability. Laurence Olivier never had what River had,' he said.

Weir also made the right choice in casting charismatic, ugly-attractive young Martha

Plimpton, daughter of actors Keith Carra-
dine and Shelley Plimpton, as Emily,
daughter of Allie Fox's equal and oppo-
site, the missionary Reverend Spellgood.
On set, in the heat and intensity of sixteen
weeks' location filming in the tiny country
of Belize, Phoenix and Plimpton fell in
love, and so began what was to be River's
longest-standing relationship.

But just as Weir observed the start of new
relationships with Phoenix's peers and co-
stars, the director also detected tensions
with the young man's family – small splits
now that would later lead to an increasingly complex, multifaceted persona. John
Phoenix was in Belize with his son as his
legally required chaperon and Weir sensed
that some of the tensions between Ford
and Phoenix in the film echoed those of
River and his father. 'With a young person
who suddenly becomes the key breadwinner

of a family,' Weir explained, 'there's an incredible amount of rearranging of things in the family hierarchy and sometimes a tension develops, particularly with the father.' And the first seeds of a double life and rebellion were being sown. While River was officially following a strict vegan diet, when his father was not around, according to Weir, 'He'd stuff himself with a Mars Bar and a Coke. It seemed a healthy steam valve.' Later in his life he would turn to stronger stuff.

*Mosquito Coast* was not a success – Harrison Ford's Allie Fox was simply too unappealing – and the year following its release was a low point for Phoenix. Driven by a need to move from wise-child to adult star, Phoenix made two false moves. First came *A Night in the Life of Jimmy Reardon*, by writer-director William Richert (later to star with Phoenix in *My*

*Own Private Idaho*). Phoenix took the lead role as the eponymous Jimmy, a seven-teen-year-old Casanova-with-problems in 1962 Chicago. An unexceptional tale of abortion, lost love, and entanglements with older women, Phoenix took the role even though his father disapproved of his character's promiscuity, and the only apparent plus points of this dubious career-move were that River established himself as a teen idol who could play sex scenes on screen, as well as a musical talent – he wrote the theme song himself.

But Phoenix, already the responsible star most teenage girls were choosing for their bedroom wall, was unhappy about the role model he was providing. By now he had a reputation as a caring, thinking, eco-conscious young man. 'A lot of people entrust themselves to you and look up to you,' Phoenix explained. 'I'm speaking about a

River Phoenix was determined that
Hollywood wouldn't change him

With Martha Plimpton

lot of teenage girls who may see the movie. I'm the monogamous type and I believe romance is important in sex, and *A Night in the Life of Jimmy Reardon* doesn't always present it that way.' He also doubted he was macho enough for the part. 'It should have starred someone a bit more masculine, like Tom Cruise,' he said.

Phoenix's second misguided move of 1987 was in Richard Benjamin's forgettable spy thriller *Little Nikita*. Second billed after Sidney Poitier, River played Jeffrey Nicholas Grant – the all-American kid about to join the air force academy who finds out his parents are Russian sleeper agents. Sidney Poitier played FBI agent Roy Parmenter, the man who breaks it to Jeff Grant that not only are his parents spies, but rogue Russian agent 'Scuba' is running amok on a murder spree with a list of fellow spies in his hands. Phoenix never stood a chance – with lines such as 'I don't know what myself is', a risible plot and some very poor teen-romance scenes, it was a performance best forgotten. Add to this Phoenix's doubts about the negative portrayal of the Russians, and the only positive thing to be gained from this movie was the experience of working with and learning from Poitier. 'He's a wonderful person and a really bright man who gave me tips about life, too, not just acting,' said the earnest adolescent.

'Let's say I took those jobs out of an insecurity, out of a feeling that I might never work again,' said Phoenix. But, together, *A Night in the Life of Jimmy Reardon* and *Little Nikita* confirmed River Phoenix not just as a teen idol worthy of cover stories on teen magazines around the world – he was also sanctified as the green lobby's official pin-up. For River, fame was worth something if he could use it to promote the causes he believed in: the conservation of rain forests, ethical treatment of animals, and care for underprivileged children. 'One thing I would like to do when I have the money is buy thousands of acres in the Brazilian rain forest and make a national park, so no one can bulldoze it to put a McDonalds there,' he told quote-hungry interviewers. 'It's a human tragedy of immense proportions. Many native Indians are losing their homes daily, and it's going to affect both you and me, because that's where most of the world's oxygen comes from.' And on behalf of the animal kingdom he expressed these views: 'One of my beliefs is about harmlessness to animals. I don't believe in eating meat or using any animal by-products or contributing to suppressing animals.' Despite his fame, he wanted no more than the simple life for himself. 'I want kids, a family of my own. I'd like to give them the first eight years of their lives in the country,' he would say.

The eco-image suited the publicity machine; the image-makers were in heaven. Here was a young actor not only possessed of a face to drool over but also prepared to expound, at any given time, everything the truth-seeking youth of the nineties most wanted to hear. No wonder teenage girls declared him to be the star they would most like to have as their boy-friend, while Britain's *Cosmopolitan*, pitched at an older age-group, elected him 'The intelligent woman's hope of what the new generation of men will be like in the twenty first century a combination of strength and sensitivity'.

# Fame

The spotlights were now switched full strength on the young actor, and they weren't always in his control. Of one photo-shoot he complained: 'I was dressed up like a model, told to pose in certain ways, to tilt my head, push my lips out, suck in my cheeks. And I'd be so tired at the end of the day, so I'd just give the damned photographer what he wanted. It was the most mortifying experience.' The young boy full of faith was beginning, ever so slightly at first, to lose his grip.

The next project, though, Sidney Lumet's *Running On Empty*, was the movie that brought River Phoenix back closer to home and confirmed him as a serious heartthrob and an actor to be reckoned with. It won him, at the tender age of seventeen, an Oscar nomination for Best Supporting Actor. With Lumet, Phoenix was once again working with a serious director who aimed for a docu-drama reality, and, while the camera was able to fall in love with his cheek-bones and retroussé nose, River was able to play to his strengths as the son of political parents on the run – the urchin with all the knowledge, sadness and wisdom of the street. Phoenix played Danny Pope, eldest son of post-sixties political radicals Arthur (Judd Hirsch) and Annie (Christine Lahti), who bombed a Government-funded napalm factory in their college days, unintentionally wounded a janitor, and found themselves on the FBI's Ten Most Wanted List. That was when Danny was two. As the film opens, Danny is seventeen, and they've been on the run ever since. All he's ever known is a life of changed names, forged documents and different coloured hair dyes. There's one more move for the family unit, and then things change; Danny is a gifted musician (a fact which allowed Phoenix to demonstrate his own prowess on the piano) and his music teacher gets him a coveted place at Juilliard. Added to that, Danny has fallen in love with Lorna Phillips, the music teacher's daughter – played by Martha Plimpton, still his steady girlfriend off screen since *Mosquito Coast*. In a pivotal scene the aspiring Romeo climbs the tree outside Lorna's window and persuades her into the night-time garden where, for the first time ever, he confesses to someone outside his family the truth about his parents. It's the first time he's allowed anyone in close, and he'd like to keep it that way. The scene where Danny cries as he tells Lorna goodbye is one of Phoenix's most moving.

As always for River Phoenix, he played the good son and comforter, the boy whose parents lean on him in troubled times, the older son who helps make things all right for his kid brother Harry (Jonas Abry). And for *Running On Empty*, River and his role were still in harmony. On this film-set, the backstage rumours revealed a serious young man, in touch with his past, grounded by the presence of girlfriend Plimpton and eager to learn. Co-star Christine Lahti was later famously to report: 'I drank a Diet Coke once, and he was furious with me. He was so adamant about clean, pure living.'

And screenwriter Naomi Foner noted both his lack of formal education and his hunger to make up for lost time. 'He was totally, totally without education,' she said. 'I mean, he could read and write, and he had an appetite for it, but he had no deep roots into any kind of sense of history or literature.' She bought him a collection of literary novels for his eighteenth birthday.

His performance as the musically gifted Danny was a *tour de force*. Sidney Lumet gave the young man fulsome praise: 'He's never studied formally but, boy, does he know how to reach inside himself.' Asked to predict Phoenix's future hopes, Lumet continued: 'I don't know what combination of things makes a star. You have to have a very strong, clear persona and you have to be a very good actor. He is both, plus he is visually beautiful. So I would say, all things being equal, he ought to have a brilliant career.'

If River was later to dabble in drugs, the habit certainly hadn't started yet. Lumet took a very hard line on drugs. 'When I speak to a young actor,' he stated, 'I just tell him or her at the start of the picture that if anything goes on I'll fire him on the spot. I'll reshoot the entire film if I have to. Aside from my moral detestation, when actors are acting under the influence of drugs, the performance may be going on in their heads but it isn't happening on screen.'

And at this stage in his career, the Phoenix family were still keeping a tight rein on their eldest son's choices of role. In publicity interviews for the film, Arlyn Phoenix talked in strict terms about Hollywood kids and drugs. 'What goes on with these

In *Running on Empty*

With his band, Aleka's Attic

kids is pathetic. Look at Drew Barrymore
. . . I saw it when she was nine years old.
You can see how kids make show business
more important than life. It's not life, it's
only a job, it's only Hollywood. Then
drugs come along and they change you
so fast you can't get a hold of yourself.
Everybody knows.' And in words which
were to prove sadly prophetic, she continued: 'Sometimes you get a script with
some of these names attached to it. I don't
even read it. I don't want to hang around
that person for two months. I don't want
to judge them. Something inside me says
something went wrong for them some-
where in order for that to happen and, but
for the grace of God, it might be River.'

And the warning signs for this vulnerable
young man, whose naïvety and other-
worldliness made him both desired by
and ill-equipped for Hollywood, were

there for those who looked. Sidney Lumet commented: 'He's incorruptible in his acting. He doesn't know how to do anything falsely. If something isn't true inside him, he just doesn't know how to do it. That can be a blessing, but it can also be a curse.' Screenwriter Naomi Foner, too, was aware of the echoes that *Running On Empty* had for River and his family at that point in his career. Foner believed Arlyn Phoenix was all too aware of the relevance of the final scenes of the movie to her own relationship with River. 'She knew that one day she would have to say goodbye to him,' explained Foner. 'I think she was saying he was ready to move on.'

*Running On Empty* garnered not only the Best Supporting Actor nomination for Phoenix, but also the Los Angeles Film Critics award for Christine Lahti as Best

Actress. Phoenix attended the sixty-first
Oscar ceremony on 29 March 1989
dressed in a tuxedo, with Martha Plimpton on his arm and his mother in atten-
dance. Phoenix lost to his future co-star
Kevin Kline's memorable performance in
*A Fish Called Wanda*, but his nomination
at such a young age made him an even
hotter property in Tinseltown. River took
it with his customary humility. 'If I have
some celebrity,' he declared, 'I hope I can
use it to make a difference. The true social
reward is that I can speak my mind and
share my thoughts about the environment
and civilization itself.'

Phoenix could now afford a little time out
to enjoy himself, so his next bit-part
brought a complete change of mood as
well as a role cannily pitched to a more
mainstream audience. 'I wanted to do
something light, pure entertainment,'

Phoenix explained, and the part of the young Indiana in the movie *Indiana Jones and the Last Crusade* was ideal.

The opening scene of this third Indy adventure fell to Phoenix. The ten minute, all-action sequence was set in Utah in the year 1912 where, in true comic-book style, a group of swarthy men hovered over a treasure trove with greedy grins on their bearded faces, watched from behind a rock by two teenage boys. One of these is the young Indiana who, discovered by the bad guys, heads off on a chase sequence which takes him from horseback to the top of a circus train full of animals, to a pit of snakes, to an encounter with a rhino and a lion – whence Indy obtains his trade-mark whip and scar on the chin. Typically, Phoenix opted to do the stunts himself. 'It would have been lying', he said, 'to have someone else do the stunts.'

The Red Hot Chili Peppers

As a pizza chef in *Love You to Death*

*Indiana Jones and the Last Crusade* was one of the biggest hits of 1989, second in box-office takings only to Tim Burton's *Batman*. Now more than ever, River Phoenix was *the* name on the lips of Hollywood's agents, but even so Phoenix turned down the lead role in George Lucas's spin-off TV series *The Young Indiana Jones Chronicles*.

# Letting Go

It was at this stage that Arlyn Phoenix saw
her opportunity to enact the next stage of
her plan for her family – a move away
from the perils of California. Hollywood
may have been providing the Phoenix
family unit with a handsome income,
but Arlyn saw no reason to succumb to
the lifestyle. 'We didn't get caught up in
the parties or the lifestyle,' she informed
the magazines. 'We saw what was happening and we said, "There's no way to raise

kids there." ' The kids had to stay, however, until a move was financially viable: 'We couldn't do it until we knew River was famous enough so that we could go away and he would still be offered parts.'

The Phoenix family moved to the environs of Gainesville, Florida, a humid, flat place of 90,000 people. They settled on a 20-acre site in the small town of Micanopy, population 600, eight miles south of the university city. 'Camp Phoenix' was custom-built for the now rich family at the end of a dirt track leading from Route 441 through Florida. A wooden house with a stream running through its land, it had three large bedrooms – one for the boys, River and Leaf, one for the girls, Rain, Summer and Liberty, and one for the parents and office use. It was reputedly filled with tapestries, Greenpeace posters and Gaia books. John Phoenix handed over the management of his son's career to Arlyn and planted an organic garden for their food.

River soon moved out to a rented house of his own – but only as far as Gainesville. The small town found him polite and unassuming – he even guested at local school workshops on the environment. But there were some far-reaching changes going on in the young star's life. His relationship with Martha Plimpton was already under strain – she was landing parts in a succession of films and they could rarely meet. (A friend of Plimpton's claimed that the actress broke off the relationship after the 1989 Oscar ceremony because she realized Phoenix was beginning to dabble in drugs.) Meanwhile River and Rainbow returned to their mutual childhood love of music and together started a band called Aleka's

Attic, in which River played guitar and wrote songs, and Rainbow sang. They rehearsed up at their parents' place, played benefits at events like Rock Against Fur and performed at a fashionable low-rent sort of place called the Hardback Café. There River soon met Suzanne Solgot, a massage therapist four years his senior, who played in an all-girl punk band and moved in to share his house.

Aleka's Attic released only one recording – a song on *Tame Yourself*, a fund-raising compilation for PETA (People for the Humane Treatment of Animals). k.d. lang and the B52s contributed to the same album and so too did REM, whose singer Michael Stripe became a close friend. Phoenix was soon said to 'idolize' Michael Balzary, a.k.a. Flea, bassist from the Red Hot Chili Peppers, and John

Frusciante, once of the same band, became another close friend. If, as many were to claim, it was the music scene that fatally introduced River Phoenix to drugs, it was now that his fate was being sealed.

For his next couple of films, Phoenix was only coasting, feeling for a direction in fully adult roles with a comedy ensemble role in Lawrence Kasdan's *I Love You to Death* (1990) and the lead in Nancy Savoca's offbeat *Dogfight* (1991). *I Love You to Death* saw River as Devo Nod, pizza cook, mystic, follower of Eastern religion, and earnest admirer of Rosalie (Tracey Ullman), wronged wife of philandering pizzeria owner Joey Boca (Kevin Kline). When harmless young Devo is drawn by his love of Rosalie to make a fumbling intervention in her attempt to murder her husband, he succeeds only in bringing the two closer together. The film

Arriving for the 1989 Poitier Award
ceremony

River lets off steam on stage

was notable only for teaming Phoenix with Keanu Reeves (who has a cameo as a bungling spaced-out would-be killer) on screen for the first time – and for the fact that, to get into character, Phoenix learned to make pizza.

River's gauche Devo didn't have a love scene and never got closer to his idolized Rosalie than reading her runes. A further shock to the fan club came with Phoenix's first leading-man role as a marine in Nancy Savoca's *Dogfight*. This was the first film where the casting of Phoenix gave the green light to the movie. (The studio was nonetheless worried that Phoenix's buzz-cut hairstyle would put off his female following, and insisted on blond highlights in his hair.)

Set in San Francisco in 1963, Phoenix plays Edward Baines Birdlace, a young marine who has been given a final night's shore liberty with his friends before shipping out to Vietnam. They decide to hold a 'dog fight', a cruel contest in which the group pool their money, rent a bar, and have a competition to see who can find the ugliest date. The marine with the best 'dog' wins the cash. Phoenix finds himself falling for his date, Rose (Lili Taylor), a plump would-be singer who writes poetry and listens to Joan Baez.

Once again, Phoenix went to great lengths to get into the part. Director Savoca arranged an abbreviated boot-camp experience for Phoenix and the other actors playing marines, and two former drill-instructors put them through their paces for four days. According to co star Anthony Clark, River got a little more into character than was necessary: 'On the first night we're out of boot camp we went to this party, and it ended up that the police were called. River was the head of that whole thing. He had a mean streak. He wanted to get into a fight. That night he was a marine.'

But if River was beginning to push himself to new horizons for his parts, it was his next role that truly took him to the edge and from which, it would seem, he never recovered. *My Own Private Idaho*, Gus Van Sant's tender, offbeat, independent movie, was the film that rocketed River Phoenix to cult stardom. His performance as a little-rent-boy-lost was to secure him his first comparisons with James Dean. Phoenix played Mike Waters, a narcoleptic lonesome hustler searching for the lost warmth of his mother's love, the truth about his never-known father, and the love of his rich-boy-taken-to-the-streets-friend Scott Favor, played by Keanu

Reeves. In parts mesmeric, in parts esoteric (Van Sant's script took the form of a
road movie with elements borrowed from
Shakespeare's *Henry IV, Part I*, its dialogue
a blend of contemporary street slang and
Shakespearean speech), *Idaho* cast its gently
hypnotic spell far from the mainstream of
movies. In one scene, a group of real-life
hustlers exchange stories in a dingy coffee
bar. In another set piece, the covers of gay
porn magazines come to life with pop-art
brio. Perhaps most memorably, Waters's
narcoleptic trances are accompanied by
fleeting images of extraordinary beauty:
leaping fish in a silver stream; a lonely
road stretching to the horizon; a bank of
quickly moving clouds; a wooden house
falling from the heavens.

Gus Van Sant wanted River Phoenix for
Waters because he sensed a part of that
character in the young actor. '*Idaho* is the

story of a rich boy who falls off the hill and a kid on the street,' Van Sant explained. 'I saw a bit of the hill in Keanu's personality and a bit of the street in River's. They played out those extensions of themselves.' Phoenix, for his part, took Van Sant's trust to heart. He worked with real-life narcoleptic Jake, the inspiration for Mike Waters, until he had a complete understanding of the curious sleep-fits. More dangerously, he researched life on the streets. Asked if he hung out with street kids in Portland, his reply was, 'Totally'. Asked how he researched the lifestyle of street hustlers he explained: 'I entered it through friends of Gus's who were already on the street, Scott and Gary. Some street kids came over to Gus's house, and we met different people at different places. But the actual street stuff was just us working on our own time. Like guerrillas. Gus's choice was to use real street guys

or us, so Keanu and I felt a great burden.'
Far from being disappointed, Phoenix's
immersion in his role was so extreme
that Van Sant feared the actor was chan-
ging into his character.

This dedication won Phoenix the Best
Actor Award at the Venice Film Festival
that year, but *Idaho* was a risky project for
someone of his star-status to take on, and
one that surely marked a diversion from
the career path chosen for him by his
parents. If it featured Phoenix taking part
in explicitly homosexual sex acts – the film
opens with Phoenix being fellated by a
balding, overweight john – it was, at heart,
a film about love. Phoenix was drawn to
the subject ('I have really strong feelings
about the search for home and mother. I
thought it was very. very touching.') and
famously contributed to the script of the
camp-fire scene, making overt his char-

*In My Own Private Idaho*

Keanu Reeves

acter's hidden needs when he murmurs to Keanu Reeves, 'I really wanna kiss you, man.' The Van Sant movie transformed him into a gay icon, but the fragility and vulnerability in his performance made audiences across the board feel protective towards him. In *Idaho* Phoenix's fragile beauty was at its most charismatic.

# Close to the Edge

If Phoenix's seductive screen aura was to survive the movie's dangers unscathed, his personal life was to pay a greater price. The truth of what happened on *My Own Private Idaho* is not known. Nobody from that film (including director Gus Van Sant) will talk. But everyone in the film business has now heard the rumours. These suggest that River's heroin-use began then, and began as a professional experiment as much as a social one – to help generate his brilliant portrait of a narcoleptic gay drug-using prostitute. *My Own Private Idaho* was an intense, collective experience. It is possible that, with Phoenix's family financially secure now, and with siblings Rainbow and Leaf also acting and contributing to the family coffer, River felt able to enjoy some kind of belated adolescent rebellion. Something certainly changed after *Idaho*.

Gus Van Sant's collaborative, experimental methods gave the young actor a glimpse beyond the mainstream to an experience he clearly preferred. Now he wanted to try a stint behind the camera, and to choose projects where he was more than just a pretty face attached to a star-status name. 'I want to buy a 16mm camera,' he declared. 'I'm not committed to the idea of being a film-maker, but I'd like to try some shorts. I really like documentaries.' And, aware of his lack of power in the movie machine, he made a deal with the Devil: one corporate monster film a year in return for the freedom to take two independent films. In what were to be the last two years of his too-short life, this led to a selection of movie roles from the banal to the bizarre.

The next movie could only have added to River's feeling of disillusionment and powerlessness. It was a far cry from *Idaho*. No doubt he had to take it to preserve his nice-kid image after his dive into the gutter. *Sneakers* (1992), directed by Phil Alden Robinson, writer–director of *Field of Dreams*, was a high-tech comedy caper about an offbeat computer–hacking security team that takes on an assignment to steal a 'black box' containing security secrets. Phoenix played nineteen-year-old Carl Arbogast, the 'kid' in an all-star

Memories of River Phoenix outside the Viper Room

Farewell messages to the much loved star.

team which had Robert Redford as its leader and Dan Aykroyd, Sidney Poitier, Ben Kingsley and Mary McDonnell as its members. Phoenix was billed above Sidney Poitier, and his coming on board was a central factor in Universal giving a green light to the movie, but apart from a couple of cute moments and an amusing comedy disco-dance routine, he barely figured in what was a forgettable, unexceptional film. Phoenix was not proud of this performance. 'I trashed myself in this,' he said. 'I've really degraded myself. He's very hyper, always twitching, the kind of guy you avoid playing if you want to walk with grace and dignity at the première.'

Unverified tales of drugged, difficult behaviour came in 1993 from the set of Phoenix's next film, Peter Bogdanovich's *The Thing Called Love*, and a glance at River Phoenix's troubled, gaunt appearance as guitar-wielding cowboy James Wright suggests they were true. Gone is the keen innocence of Phoenix's earlier roles. In its place is a misjudged, overbearing performance.

The film told the tale of four young Country and Western musicians trying to make a breakthrough in Nashville. Phoenix's James Wright is battling with Kyle (Dermot Mulroney, who was also to co-star in Phoenix's next project, *Silent Tongue*) for the heart of Miranda (Samantha Mathis). Phoenix was showcased live singing and playing guitar, and wrote a song for the movie, 'Lone Star State of Mind'. But even though it was his name on the cast-list that persuaded Paramount to give the project the go-ahead, Phoenix's performance struck a discordant note.

There was, though, plenty going on off-screen. 'He was crazy about Samantha right away,' said Peter Bogdanovich. 'He was anxious to have lots of kissing scenes. He was saying, "In the lovemaking scene, can we really do it? Can you just put us in there, close the door and let us go?" He was only half-kidding.' Samantha Mathis was to be the woman with whom he was to have his last relationship, and who was with him when he died. Despite his new-found love, however, his drug abuse on location in Tennessee was so serious that one night's filming featuring Phoenix was reportedly unusable.

An interview from the set, published posthumously in the British newspaper the *Mail on Sunday*, gives a stark insight into River Phoenix's rapidly deteriorating state. Tom Daniels was shocked by Phoenix's unkempt appearance ('He looked like a twenty-three-year-old who had been up all night.') and by his rambling, shivering and incoherence. His conversation was riddled with confusion and distress. 'I am being jerked around in the way you're always jerked around,' he told Daniels. 'They want you to do what they want you to do. I have twenty personalities on top of the ten I already have. So now I have thirty people in my head.' He made no attempt to disguise his unhappiness ('I sleep and I work and that's it. I don't do anything fun for myself. I have to immerse myself or I feel false.') or his growing frustration: 'Sometimes I do a take to pacify executives and it winds up in the movie and I'm kicking myself.'

It was whispered knowledge on the set of *The Thing Called Love* that Phoenix was a mixed-up kid who had had what was vaguely referred to as a drug problem.

But friends say no one with any power in the industry enquired too deeply into just how mixed-up he was for fear of upsetting the money machine of his image as a sexy saint. At the end, friends say he just gave in to the drugs, trying to disguise the creeping clues to his abuse – the bloodshot eyes, the incoherence, the fragile frame – by working out at a gym with a personal trainer.

He became edgy and moody. At parties, he would just play his own 'original compositions' on the guitar. At a wedding at which even the Red Hot Chili Peppers conformed and wore tuxedos, Phoenix turned up in sneakers, ripped shorts and a dirty T-shirt. A British actor living in Hollywood testified to Phoenix's heavy use of cocaine. The actor would call Phoenix at the St James's Club, a grand white 1930s apartment block turned hotel which River frequented, and they would meet to drink vodka and snort and free-base cocaine. 'Charles' was also testing the liquid designer-drug GHB – Gamma Hydroxybutric acid – much discussed in reports of River's death, and which had previously hit headlines when it caused rocker Billy Idol to collapse in convulsions. 'Charles' never saw Phoenix use it but Taki, columnist on the English magazine the *Spectator*, has quoted an actress friend's account of a visit from Phoenix which includes his use of GHB as well as cocaine and morphine.

# Too Much Too Young

It must have been the increasingly dark side of Phoenix's nature that chose his last complete role as Talbot Roe in Sam Shepard's Wild West ghost story, *Silent Tongue* (1993). When Talbot Roe's half-Indian wife Awbonnie dies in childbirth, he becomes crazed with grief and sits in lonely vigil in the middle of a desolate prairie guarding her body in a burial tree. Most of River's time on screen is spent rolling his eyes and howling. A suitably macabre final bow.

For the six weeks just before his death, River had been out on location in the desert, 300 miles south of Salt Lake City, near a little town called Torrey. He was filming *Dark Blood*, another of his esoteric movie choices, full of caves, candles and soliloquies against the sky, which had Jonathan Pryce and Judy Davis as city types in an encounter with Phoenix's alternately charming and terrifying character called only Boy.

Directed by Dutch art-house director George Sluizer, whose 1988 chiller *Spoorloos (The Vanishing)* brought him a crossover into Hollywood, the production was not a happy one. Jonathan Pryce recalled premonitions of disaster during the filming. 'River said, "Somebody's going to die on this film." We were on this kind of inexorable journey to disaster.

Every day there was some kind of diffi-
culty. It just seemed as if something had to
give.' Phoenix phoned William Richert
from the set and left a message on his
answering machine: 'I'm out here in
Utah and I'm having a kind of hard time
keeping my head above water in this crazy
business.'

The location work over, Phoenix went
back to Los Angeles to start on scenes set
inside the hut where Boy lived. He was
put up in the Nikko hotel on La Cienega
Boulevard – a big Japanese business hotel
with a waterfall and much marble in its
lobby. He worked on the Saturday, but he
had Sunday off, so he was going to have
fun. (He was never to return, the half-
complete movie had to be scrapped, and,
in two separate lawsuits by insurance and
production companies, his estate was to be
sued after his death to the tune of $5.5

million for breach of contract due to the use of illegal drugs.)

Hotel witnesses confirm that Phoenix and his friends had started partying early that Sunday. Room service delivered drinks and food and noted the chaos, the loud music and the spaced-out look on Phoenix's face. They knew it was a drugs high, but they still brought the drinks. At 10.30p.m. Phoenix asked that his car be brought round. He and his friends made a rowdy exit from the hotel lobby. Someone else drove while River slumped in the back.

They were on their way to the Viper, where Phoenix and his friends, some of whom were part of Aleka's Attic, were intending to jam with other musicians. At the club, River was joined by his brother Leaf, his sister Rain and his girlfriend

Samantha Mathis. They sat at a table off the dance floor and ordered drinks. A waitress noted that River was stoned on arrival: 'He was barely able to stand, and he kept leaping up and bumping into things. His words were so blurred you could hardly understand him.'

Eyewitness reports give conflicting evidence of the final hours of River's short life. Some claim Phoenix went to a small room behind the stage with a friend and shot up a speedball – the same lethal combination of heroin and cocaine that killed John Belushi eleven years before. Others say River stayed seated and threw back glass after glass of highly potent German Jägermeister. Another story has him dancing around the room in a frenzy of activity, while a rare on-the-record account from club regular Heather McDougal claims there was nothing at

all unusual about Phoenix's behaviour
that night.

But everyone at the Viper on that fateful
night agrees on the sequence of events that
filled River's last minutes at the club.
Sitting at the table, Phoenix became
terribly ill and began to vomit over himself. His friends took him to the washroom
to clean him up. They splashed cold water
on his face and tried to stop him trem-
bling; then they got him back to the table.
By now he was showing serious signs of an
overdose. He began having seizures and
then he slumped and slid under the table.
Fighting for breath, he asked to be taken
to fresh air. Leaf, Rain and Samantha
Mathis helped him outside (some say that
on his way out he called out, 'I'm going to
die, dude.') and there on the pavement in
the dark hours of Hallowe'en the fragile
young star who still had so much promise

played out his death in the full glare of publicity.

The circumstances puzzled police and were investigated by homicide detectives. 'There's no way of knowing what precipitated his death,' said Bill Martin, a spokesman for the Los Angeles County Sheriff's Department. The police were called in 'because it is unusual for someone of that age to die like this'. But the investigation ruled out any foul play. A coroner's report found no signs of needle marks on River's body, and concluded that the drugs which killed him had been either 'inhaled or ingested'.

How did it happen? River Phoenix was known as one of the most clean-living stars in Hollywood. He was, famously, a strict teetotaller and vegan who used nothing that originated from animals –

including eggs, cheese and honey. His mother, Arlyn, would whip up tofu scrambles for him on set. His only vice was to have taken up smoking chemical-free organic tobacco. The family thrived on veganism and the avoidance of modern medicine. 'I've refused to have them inoculated,' Arlyn said. 'I've never given them an aspirin. If some awful illness happened in our family . . . then I'd look at it as a challenge to heal ourselves with herbs and spiritual enlightenment.' River was the child of people with an uncompromising, if benign, ideology of alternative living.

In his later years, though, he struck out on a different, more dangerous path. Everyone is keen to pass the buck for what happened. The film industry is keen to blame Phoenix's musical connections for his death – everyone knows, they say, that in LA's music clubs, a favourite hang-out for the young, hip and cool, drugs circulate freely among the clientele. Still others point a finger at River's 'pushy' mother Arlyn – who now prefers to be known as 'Heart' – for bequeathing her eldest son an impossible burden.

Certainly the breach between River Phoenix's uneducated faith and the Hollywood machine which grasped his ideals and spat them out as so many press releases proved too great. As a chasm opened between his private and public life, River lost his footing. 'I am confused,' he told his ever-hungry interviewers. 'I go back and forth about success and wealth and want to take the Devil's bribe and use it for God.' He still spoke of founding a home for abused kids, the homeless, the psychotics, of opening a theatre in a small town, of setting up a touring educational seminar group. He succeeded in buying 800 acres of forest on the border of Panama and Costa Rica. But he had to push his true self further and further from sight. 'Depending on the interviewer and the publication, I lie all the time,' he told Britain's *Time Out*. 'They'll change the truth anyhow so I may as well say what I like. I am a kind of minute commodity, my name is no longer my own.' His only refuge was to immerse himself in the make-believe of his roles – or drugs.

There was a small private memorial service for River Phoenix in Hollywood. Among the close friends who spoke at his memorial were directors Peter Bogdanovich and Rob Reiner, actresses Helen Mirren and Christine Lahti, *Running On Empty* writer Naomi Foner, River's agent Iris Burton, his sisters Rain and Liberty, and his nineteen-year-old brother Summer. River's mother spoke the final tribute and laid him to rest. Leaf, who was with him when he died, and his father John chose to remain at home in Florida with his ashes. River had been cremated the week before. Flea from the Red Hot Chili Peppers, REM singer Stipe and actor Dan Aykroyd were there. There was singing and dancing.

River's death not only left behind the films he did, but what might have been. There were parts lined up into the future, many of them continuing Phoenix's descent into the darker side of life. He was due to start shooting the pivotal role of the Interviewer, Daniel, in the Tom Cruise vehicle *Interview with the Vampire* on 30 November (the recasting of this role brought another posthumous lawsuit to the tune of $500,000); John Boorman was going to feature him alongside Sean Connery and Winona Ryder in *Broken*

*Dreams*; there was to be a part in the film of Dennis Cooper's grotesque tale *Frisk*; Gus Van Sant, whose recent *Even Cowgirls Get the Blues* had featured a cameo from Phoenix, was likely to cast him as the young Andy Warhol in a biopic. And, what no doubt seemed most important to River himself, at the time of his death Phoenix had fifteen songs on a demo tape and was close to signing a record contract.

But all this would only ever exist in the imaginations of his bereft fans. A small dedicated group kept a vigil outside the Viper, bringing flowers and burning candles to a pavement altar. 'A true individual who will be remembered,' said one note; 'The Eternal River Flows' read an inscription on a water-colour.

The man-child of great beauty and seriousness was gone, but not forgotten.